Currie

by Iain Gray

Lang**Syne**
PUBLISHING
WRITING *to* REMEMBER

Lang**Syne**

PUBLISHING

WRITING *to* REMEMBER

Vineyard Business Centre,
Pathhead, Midlothian EH37 5XP
Tel: 01875 321 203 Fax: 01875 321 233
E-mail: info@lang-syne.co.uk
www.langsyneshop.co.uk

Design by Dorothy Meikle
Printed by Ricoh Print Scotland
© Lang Syne Publishers Ltd 2010

ISBN 978-1-85217-224-4

Currie

Currie

MOTTO:
Inspire to victory.

CREST:
A crown surmounted by a lion's head.

TERRITORY:
Balilone, on Bute.

Chapter one:

The origins of the clan system

by Rennie McOwan

The original Scottish clans of the Highlands and the great families of the Lowlands and Borders were gatherings of families, relatives, allies and neighbours for mutual protection against rivals or invaders.

Scotland experienced invasion from the Vikings, the Romans and English armies from the south. The Norman invasion of what is now England also had an influence on land-holding in Scotland. Some of these invaders stayed on and in time became 'Scottish'.

The word clan derives from the Gaelic language term 'clann', meaning children, and it was first used many centuries ago as communities were formed around tribal lands in glens and mountain fastnesses.

The format of clans changed over the centuries, but at its best the chief and his family held the land on behalf of all, like trustees, and the ordinary clansmen and women believed they had a blood relationship with the founder of their clan.

There were two way duties and obligations. An inadequate chief could be deposed and replaced by someone of greater ability.

Clan people had an immense pride in race. Their relationship with the chief was like adult children to a father and they had a real dignity.

The concept of clanship is very old and a more feudal notion of authority gradually crept in.

Pictland, for instance, was divided into seven principalities ruled by feudal leaders who were the strongest and most charismatic leaders of their particular groups.

By the sixth century the 'British' kingdoms of Strathclyde, Lothian and Celtic Dalriada (Argyll) had emerged and Scotland, as one nation, began to take shape in the time of King Kenneth MacAlpin.

Some chiefs claimed descent from

ancient kings which may not have been accurate in every case.

By the twelfth and thirteenth centuries the clans and families were more strongly brought under the central control of Scottish monarchs.

Lands were awarded and administered more and more under royal favour, yet the power of the area clan chiefs was still very great.

The long wars to ensure Scotland's independence against the expansionist ideas of English monarchs extended the influence of some clans and reduced the lands of others.

Those who supported Scotland's greatest king, Robert the Bruce, were awarded the territories of the families who had opposed his claim to the Scottish throne.

In the Scottish Borders country - the notorious Debatable Lands - the great families built up a ferocious reputation for providing warlike men accustomed to raiding into England and occasionally fighting one another.

Chiefs had the power to dispense justice

and to confiscate lands and clan warfare produced a society where martial virtues - courage, hardiness, tenacity - were greatly admired.

Gradually the relationship between the clans and the Crown became strained as Scottish monarchs became more orientated to life in the Lowlands and, on occasion, towards England.

The Highland clans spoke a different language, Gaelic, whereas the language of Lowland Scotland and the court was Scots and in more modern times, English.

Highlanders dressed differently, had different customs, and their wild mountain land sometimes seemed almost foreign to people living in the Lowlands.

It must be emphasised that Gaelic culture was very rich and story-telling, poetry, piping, the clarsach (harp) and other music all flourished and were greatly respected.

Highland culture was different from other parts of Scotland but it was not inferior or less sophisticated.

Central Government, whether in London

"The spirit of the clan means much to thousands of people"

or Edinburgh, sometimes saw the Gaelic clans as a challenge to their authority and some sent expeditions into the Highlands and west to crush the power of the Lords of the Isles.

Nevertheless, when the eighteenth century Jacobite Risings came along the cause of the Stuarts was mainly supported by Highland clans.

The word Jacobite comes from the Latin for James - Jacobus. The Jacobites wanted to restore the exiled Stuarts to the throne of Britain.

The monarchies of Scotland and England became one in 1603 when King James VI of Scotland (1st of England) gained the English throne after Queen Elizabeth died.

The Union of Parliaments of Scotland and England, the Treaty of Union, took place in 1707.

Some Highland clans, of course, and Lowland families opposed the Jacobites and supported the incoming Hanoverians.

After the Jacobite cause finally went down at Culloden in 1746 a kind of ethnic cleansing took place. The power of the chiefs was curtailed. Tartan and the pipes were banned in law.

Many emigrated, some because they wanted to, some because they were evicted by force. In addition, many Highlanders left for the cities of the south to seek work.

Many of the clan lands became home to sheep and deer shooting estates.

But the warlike traditions of the clans and the great Lowland and Border families lived on, with their descendants fighting bravely for freedom in two world wars.

Remember the men from whence you came, says the Gaelic proverb, and to that could be added the role of many heroic women.

The spirit of the clan, of having roots, whether Highland or Lowland, means much to thousands of people.

Chapter two:

Warrior poets

Currie is an unusual surname in that it can be traced back to no less than four separate sources, and proud bearers of the name have made a significant contribution to the rich tapestry of Scotland's often turbulent history.

One source is the Scottish Gaelic 'coire', meaning a cauldron, and which is the root of the place name of Corrie, a parish in Dumfriesshire.

Also from the Scottish Gaelic is 'curagh', 'curragh', or 'currach', meaning a bog or a mossy dell, while from the ancient Brythonic there is the word 'curi', meaning a hollow.

The present day affluent Edinburgh suburb of Currie, for example, located about six miles from the centre of the Scottish capital, is thought to stem from Brythonic roots.

Variations of the name include Curry and Currey, but Currie is the most common form of the name found in Scotland.

Much of the high drama and romance associated with the name stem from roots that lie deep under the ancient soils of the Highlands and Islands, with Currie being the anglicised version of MacMhuirich, or MacMureach, meaning 'son of Mhuirich', and pronounced 'MacVurich'.

Other Gaelic forms include MacMuirediach, and it was a Muirediach O'Daly, who lived from 1180 to 1222, who is regarded as the progenitor, or 'name father', of what became the noted clan of MacMhuirich, or Murrich.

Today, as Clan Currie, they boast the proud motto of 'Inspire to victory', and their crest is a crown surmounted by a lion's head.

This crown refers to the clan's descent, through Muirediach O'Daly, from the gloriously named Conn of the Hundred Battles, the 110th High King of Ireland and who ruled in the late first century.

Muirediach O'Daly was recognised as one of the most gifted bards, or poets, of his time, serving as bard to the court of Cathal Crodhearg of Connaught, and bards such as Muirediach occupied a prominent and highly respected place in the community of clans of both Ireland and Scotland.

Their role was not merely to entertain their kinsfolk with songs and poetry, but to act as the custodians of the clan's heritage and traditions and complex genealogy.

This ancient Celtic bardic tradition stretched back through the mists of time to the Druids, when the bards formed an elite within the clan structure, along with those skilled in what were then considered the arcane and black arts of astronomy and medicine.

Muirediach O'Daly, in addition to his renowned skills as a bard, also appears to have possessed a rather fiery temperament, and was forced to flee his native Ireland and seek refuge in Scotland in 1213 after he split the skull of a steward of the powerful chief of Clan O'Donnell with one mighty blow of a battleaxe.

The steward had incurred his wrath after demanding that he pay rent to the O'Donnell chief: through custom and tradition, the rather pampered bards were not expected to pay for anything – least of all rent to a rival chief.

Unrepentant, and in true bardic tradition, the bold Muirediach promptly wrote a poem about his feat!

Settling on the island of Islay, in the Inner Hebrides, Muirediach's fame as a bard had spread before him and he was warmly welcomed into the court of Donald, Lord of the Isles.

While Donald became the name father of the mighty Clan Donald, or MacDonald, Muirediach became the founder of what became Clan MacMhuirich, and the clan was honoured with the office of hereditary bards and historians to the Lords of the Isles.

An important duty of the bard in times of conflict was to not only summon his clan to arms, but to inspire them to victory through war chants and reciting poems of past glorious deeds – and this explains the Currie motto of 'Inspire to Victory'.

One of these epic war poems was recited

on the eve of one of the most savage battles on
Scottish soil - the battle of Harlaw, fought on
July 24, 1411, just north of Aberdeen.

Also known as the battle of Red Harlaw,
because of the blood spilled, it occurred after
Donald Macdonald, 2nd Lord of the Isles, had
mustered about 6000 of his best clansmen and
burned Inverness after crossing to the mainland
and marching up the Great Glen.

His strength swelled to 10,000 after other
clansmen including Camerons, Chattans,
MacIntoshes, and MacLeods joined him.
Promising them rich pickings, Macdonald
marched them towards Aberdeen.

The Earl of Mar hastily assembled a
force that included northeast lairds, while the
Provost of Aberdeen also raised men.

The opposing forces met just north of
Aberdeen, and battle was joined shortly after the
summer sun had risen.

Before the battle, however, Lachlann
Mor MacMhuirrich, bard to the Lord of the Isles,
exhorted his clansmen to furious combat with

epic lines that included:

> O' Children of Conn of the
>   Hundred Battles,
> Now is the time for you to win
>   recognition.
> O' raging whelps,
> O' sturdy heroes,
> O' most sprightly lions,
> O' battle-loving warriors,
> O' brave firebrands,
> The Children of Conn of the
>   Hundred Battles.
> O' Children of Conn,
>   remember,
> Hardihood in time of battle

Inspired by the bard's exhortation, the fearless and ferocious clansmen repeatedly charged the ranks of the Earl of Mar and his men, only to be cut down in swathes, but not before exacting their own toll in blood.

As the sun sank low in the west, both sides were exhausted and had to retire from the fray, leaving behind a battlefield littered with the corpses of at least 1000 clansmen and 600 of Mar's men.

The fate of the Curries was inextricably linked to that of the MacDonald Lords of the Isles, who, as masters of a sprawling fiefdom, ruled a confederacy of clans that included Macquarries, Macleans, Macfies, Macleods, MacNeils, and Mackinnons.

From their base at Dunyveg on the south of Islay, they controlled a strategic sea route between the north of Ireland and Scotland's western seaboard.

Ruling as virtual monarchs in their own right, and with a motto of 'By sea and by land' and crest of a mailed fist grasping a cross, it was not until 1476 that John of the Isles was forced to accept the authority of the Crown.

This incurred the wrath of his volatile and bastard son, John, who raised rebellion against both his own father and James III, winning a famous victory over them in 1481 at the Battle of Badh na Fala (Bloody Bay), near Tobermory, on Mull.

By 1493 the situation had reached such a stage of anarchy, with royal authority being flouted at every turn, that James IV finally annexed the Lordship of the Isles to the Crown, with the monarch himself assuming the title of Lord of the Isles.

Chapter three:

For the Stuart cause

With the power of the MacDonald Lords of the Isles shattered, the Curries appear to have split into two groups.

John MacMhuirich, who was chief of his clan at the time of the fall of the Lordship of the Isles, already held lands in Kintyre, and it was from here that he fought a vain battle to restore the lordship.

His son, Donald, acquired lands at Balilone, in Bute, and it is the Curries of Balilone who are recognised today as the senior branch of the clan.

In 1491, however, before the eventual break-up of the Lordship of the Isles, Niall MacMhuirich offered his bardic skills to the MacDonalds of Clanranald, on South Uist, and his descendants became responsible for producing one of the largest collections of Gaelic poetry in existence, particularly the famed Red Book of Clanranald.

Another Niall MacMhuirich, born in 1637, and who died in 1726, wrote what was to become the final collection in Scotland of Gaelic prose written in the ancient style: this was a colourful chronicle of the military campaign of James Graham, 1st Marquis of Montrose.

A bitter civil war raged in Scotland between 1638 and 1649 between the forces of those Presbyterian Scots who had signed a National Covenant that opposed the divine right of the Stuart monarchy and Royalists such as Montrose, whose prime allegiance was to Charles I.

Although he had initially supported the Covenant, his conscience later forced him to switch sides and the period from 1644 to 1645 became known as the Year of Miracles because of Montrose's brilliant military successes.

He won a great victory at the battle of Inverlochy, on February 2, 1645, when the Earl of Argyll was forced to flee in his galley after 1,500 of his Covenanters were wiped out in a surprise attack, followed by victory at Kilsyth on August 15, 1645.

He was finally defeated at Philiphaugh, near Selkirk, however, less than a month later.

The MacDonalds of Clanranald, whose famed stronghold was Castle Tioram on South Uist, continued to prove loyal to the cause of the Royal House of Stuart, not least during the Jacobite Rising of 1745, along with their Currie kinsfolk.

The prince had landed on the small Outer Hebridean island of Eriskay on July 22, 1745, landing on the mainland at Loch nan Uamh three days later.

The first clan chief he had appealed to for support was the Clanranald Chief, Ranald MacDonald and, although he reluctantly refused to raise his clansmen his son, Young Clanranald, raised some of the clan's cadet branches.

Fifty of Young Clanranald's men formed the bodyguard that accompanied the prince on August 19 to Glenfinnan, on Loch Shiel, where the Jacobite Standard was raised.

They were later joined by more than 150 other Clanranald MacDonalds.

Along with the Keppoch regiment, the MacDonald of Clanranald Regiment took the town of Dundee, and later fought with distinction at the battle of Prestonpans, positioned on the right wing of the front line of the Jacobite army.

This honour had first been accorded to the clan by the great warrior king Robert the Bruce at the battle of Bannockburn in 1314.

Victory was achieved at the battle of Prestonpans in September, and in October the confident prince and his army set off from Edinburgh on the long march south to London in October, to claim what was believed to be the rightful Stuart inheritance of the throne.

The army reached only as far as Derby, however, before the controversial decision was taken in early December to withdraw back over the border.

Jacobite hopes were later dashed forever at the battle of Culloden, fought on Drummossie Moor, near Inverness, on April 16, 1746.

In what was the last major battle fought

on British soil, hundreds of clansmen died on the battlefield while hundreds of others died later from their wounds and the brutal treatment of their government captors.

The MacDonalds of Clanranald and their kinsfolk such as the Curries suffered particularly heavy casualties, and Young Clanranald himself was severely wounded.

As the hereditary bards of the MacDonalds of Clanranald - whose motto is 'My hope is constant in thee', and whose crest is a hand emerging from a castle turret, wielding a sword - the Curries are recognised as one of their septs, and entitled to share in their heritage and traditions and adopt their tartan.

There is a separate Currie tartan, however, that was first created in 1822 for the visit of George IV to Scotland.

It was then that Lord Alexander MacDonald, the Chief of Clan Donald, granted James Currie of Balilone and Garrochoran permission to use the Lord of the Isles tartan as the basis for his family tartan.

The grant allowed the incorporation of black and gold colours from Currie's own coat-of-arms into the Lord of the Isles tartan, 'to constitute a guard to the darker green square of the basic Lord of the Isles tartan.'

The grant was reconfirmed in 1972 and, until 1991, the tartan could only be worn by Curries of the Balilone and Garrochoran line, but was finally adopted as the official clan tartan a year later.

A Clan Currie Society flourishes today, promoting not only their own proud heritage and traditions in particular, but that of Scotland in general: in 2001, for example, it was the leading sponsor of all Scottish clans for the National Tartan Day ceremonies in Washington D.C.

There is a common misconception that the Curries of the Western Isles are linked to the equally proud Clan MacPherson.

The confusion exists because the MacPhersons are sometimes known as Clan Mhurrich – but the 'Mhurrich' who was the clan's name father was a 12th century abbot of

Kingussie, not the Mhurrich, or Muirediach,
who was the progenitor of the Curries of the
Western Isles.

Chapter four:

Honours and fame

In the centuries following Culloden, Curries were still to be found on the battlefield, where many achieved distinction.

General Arthur Currie, born in Napperton, Ontario, in 1875, and who was among the most successful Allied generals during the First World War, is still regarded as one of the finest commanders in Canadian military history.

His fellow Canadian, Major David Currie, who was born in 1912 and died in 1986, was awarded the Victoria Cross during the Second World War for his actions in Normandy in command of a battle group of tanks from the South Alberta Regiment, along with artillery and infantry of the Argyll and Sutherland Highlanders.

Colonel William McMurdo Currie, born in Glasgow in 1916, and known affectionately in his lifetime as 'Colonel Bill', was the 22nd Laird of Balilone and the 30th Chief of Clan MacMhuirrich.

Educated at both the Glasgow School of Art and the Royal College of Science and Technology (now Strathclyde University), he had a distinguished war record, serving throughout the Second World War in the clandestine 'special services' and being cited for several acts of bravery.

His glittering military honours included the French *Croix de Guerre de Allies*, the Tunisian *Order of Glory*, and the Polish *Virtuti Militari*.

A keen historian and genealogist, he was a Fellow of both the Society of Antiquaries of Scotland and the Royal Celtic Society and, in 1959, founded in Glasgow the first Clan Currie Society.

In 1990, two years before his death, he was made a *Knight of the White Eagle* – Poland's highest state order.

Before his death, Colonel Currie, the last of the Balilone line, named American-born

Robert Currie as his successor, with the title of Clan Commander.

This was in recognition of his re-establishment of the Clan Currie Society as the cultural and educational organisation that it is today.

In the world of literature, James Currie was the great biographer and friend of Scotland's national bard, Robert Burns. Born at Kirkpatrick-Fleming, in Dumfriesshire, in 1756, he published his *Life of Burns* in 1800, four years after the poet's death.

Taking to the skies, Dr Nancy Currie, born in Wilmington, Delaware, in 1958, is the American astronaut who was assigned from the army to the N.A.S.A. Johnson Space Center in 1987 as a flight simulator engineer in the space shuttle training aircraft.

An astronaut since 1990, she has flown on four space shuttle missions, and, at the time of writing, has amassed an impressive 1000 hours in space.

In the realm of politics, Edwina Currie, who was born Edwina Cohen in Liverpool in

1946, is the former British Conservative party politician and Junior Health Minister who is probably now best known for her revelation in 2002 that she had had a four-year affair with Conservative Prime Minister John Major.

In the world of sport, John Curry, born in Birmingham in 1949 and who died in 1994, three years after being diagnosed with AIDS, was the figure skater who won both the Olympic and World Championships in 1976.

Curries and Currys are also well represented in the world of entertainment.

American-born Adam Curry is the broadcasting and Internet personality who has played a key role in the development and promotion of pod casting, while Ann Curry, born in Guam in 1956 but raised in Oregon, is a leading American journalist and television personality.

On the stage, Finlay Currie, born in Edinburgh in 1878 and who died in 1968, is the former organist, music hall singer, and choirmaster who is now recognised as one of the greatest character actors of all time.

With his trademark craggy features he appeared in movies such as *Ben-Hur*, *The Fall of the Roman Empire*, *Whisky Galore*, and *Billy Liar*.

In contemporary times, Tim Curry is the Cheshire-born actor, singer and composer best known for his role as the mad scientist Dr Frank N. Furter in the 1975 *The Rocky Horror Show*.

Justin Currie, born in Glasgow in 1964, is the singer/songwriter and founder member of the highly successful band Del Amitri. Hits penned by Currie include *Nothing Ever Happens* and *Always the Last to Know*.

In the world of art, Ken Currie, born in 1960, is the Scottish-based artist who is considered one of the world's most imaginative figurative painters.